The Bold and Beautiful Bunnies of Jericho Beach

The Bold and Beautiful Bunnies of Jericho Beach

Rowena Kong

Annie Ho

2022

ISBN: 9781990782251

Jericho beach is situated in the West Point Grey neighbourhood of Vancouver in the Western Canadian province of British Columbia. It is a beloved nature's retreat in a laidback city where flora and fauna thrive amidst regular cycling, water sports and leisure activities enjoyed by local enthusiastic visitors. It is designated a sensitive ecological area and migrating birds like the snow geese can be seen grazing in its field in late autumn. In addition to birds and squirrels, both the young and old beachgoers have come to appreciate another kind of unlikely mammal residents which have, over the decade, called Jericho beach park their seemingly permanent home. They are the vulnerable yet resilient bunny rabbits which have populated the beach since pet owners began leaving their unwanted bunnies on the beach. Beautiful but bold, these sweet little ones brave the mildly harsh natural living conditions day after day and begin to adapt and overcome, not without a price or compromise on their health and hygiene. If they are fortunate enough, a human visitor may bring along a carrot and veggie treat to satisfy their hunger pangs. Otherwise, they may have to fend for themselves and survive solely on plain grass in the fields. When the wild blackberries ripen in summer, these bunnies are blessed with another destined source of nutrition as they feed on them. Nevertheless, a keen observer will notice that those certain wild blackberry bushes where more of these sweet bunnies hide and live under are especially fruitful, laden with plentiful colorful berries dangling from their stalks during their summer ripening season more than other places in Vancouver. The reason being that the rabbits' droppings provide useful natural fertilizer for the berry plants in a very special way, thus creating a mutually beneficial yearly life cycle that is less obvious to the casual visitor. In a unique manner, the bunnies help contribute to the productivity of the wild flora, particularly the berry-bearing ones at Jericho beach. These lovely new settlers are not there simply to take up space and send trouble as most would have thought in the first place. Beach visitors who come here to pick the berries for themselves might never have thought that the reason their berries taste better is all thanks to these little unexpected helpers.

Of course, unlike humans, these sweeties are easily contented with their unfortunate fate in exchange for a new gift of freedom. These beautiful homeless bunnies abandoned by pet owners do not belong to the wild type species, contrary to what was stated on the signs put up around the beach area. As a natural eco-habitat, Jericho beach became the voluntary residence for these bunnies who needed to learn to live in an uncared-for environment. The stronger ones triumph over nutrition shortages, lack of affection, and risk of predators. However, some suffer from poor hygienic conditions of dry sandy grounds and environmental allergens, not to mention malnutrition. Without regular provision of clean drinking water, a number of them succumb to skin problems and related ailments.

Challenges aside, the population of bunnies here has been quite stable over the years, with new kits being born each new season. Interestingly, these bunnies can create their own segregation based on their niches on the opposite East and West sides of the wide beach territory. With lush greenery and abundance of fresh grass available in Jericho East, the bunnies which are used to settling in this area are more independent but less sociable with human visitors. In the West side, the opposite is true. Faced with lack of food where the grounds are blanketed with dry beach sand, it is not a rare chance to encounter a bunny eagerly standing up on its feet and lifting its paws to plead with you for a treat. When fortunate enough to receive one, you can tell how grateful and glad it is.

1 "May I have a treat or two?"

2A Jericho West side bunny digging the ground by the beach's popular sailing club.

3A somewhat "self-sufficient" bunny surrounded by refreshing greens on the East side of Jericho beach park.

4Sick bunnies braving the hurt from skin and fur problems with the help of being fed fresh veggies.

5Deserving attention and care, yet receiving none. This bunny has both eye and skin problems that would have benefitted from a mobile veterinary service, should this be possible in the future.

Snow-white albino bunnies are quite rare compared to the major population of black bunnies here, but it is not impossible to encounter them. The baby albino above is one of a pair of twins spotted in the late summer of 2018. It is natural for baby bunnies to be extremely fearful and aversive of humans during their first few weeks of life as this one is particularly so. It was another near impossible task to trail after it for too long with the great speed it would race away from perceived potential predators. Fortunately, this elusive snow-white lingered for a considerable time to be fed some nutritious kale when there were mature black bunnies in its close company

6"Sharing some kale with someone who might be my Mommy..."

7This is a lovely and sociable brown male bunny which we get to affectionately nicknamed "Laenie." He spends most of his time on Jericho West and loves kale. Laenie is active and quick-witted, always hopping towards us whenever we visit him with plenty of treats. As expected, he is popular with his fellow bunnies and enjoys the attention they offer him. In the following photograph, Laenie can be seen sweetly sharing a carrot with his black bunny companion.

A white-gray baby bunny in this left photograph was born in the summer of 2018. It is nicknamed "Gerry" and has a sweet and gentle personality. Gerry, again like Laenie, lives on the West side of Jericho beach. Although Gerry's niche was at first about metres away from Laenie's niche, Gerry came to join Laenie and his gang which is closer to the sailing club towards the fall of 2018.

8A young Gerry enjoying a carrot treat.

9Gerry at about a few months old

As time goes by, with these brave and resilient bunnies, and new generations counting, getting used to their lives in the environment of Jericho beach, it may be unwise to ultimately displace them away from their natural abode. It is also likely that such scenario would not happen in near future due to the lack of concern and attention paid to these strong little ones. Local rabbit shelters are also short on space, funds and resources to accommodate these poor abandoned bunnies. It would make the fate of these bunnies worse should those shelters attempt to receive them. They also risked being endangered one day due to the heavy spaying and neutering practised under the care of these rabbit shelters. Here at the beach, these free bunnies can safely reproduce and nurture their precious offspring as they choose and we are blessed with adorable baby bunnies year after year. Perhaps,

Jericho beach is not as bad a home after all for these courageous sweethearts as one would have thought in the first place.

10"Mmmm...This kale is tastier than dried grass..."

Figure 11 Baby bunnies are born many in the summer, though cool mild weather with moderate heat is preferred by these...

Figure 12 "Peeping at me?"

Figure 13 "We'll share side by side..."

Figure 14 A cute brownie takes its shelter and looks on under the protective cover of a bush.

Figure 15 Bright and beautiful, but with its eyes hurt, this bunny endures the unspeakable pain and is contented with a light green meal

Figure 16 "Even a sweet and chewy banana is worth me going for!"

Figure 17Bearing its sufferings and pain courageously, this sick bunny has developed lumps in its body, yet invincible enough to raise itself up to gather sweet blackberries to feed itself for survival. Impressive and admirable!

Happiness is a Bunny

Happiness is receiving a bright orange carrot when I am waiting for a treat.

Happiness is still being able to feast on this juicy kale in spite of my sore eyes and pain...

Happiness is gathering a bunch of hay for my summer afternoon moments.

Happiness is smartly posing for my visitor's camera and having my photos taken.

Happiness is sharing a bright long carrot with my friendly playmates.

Happiness is digging my comfortable rabbit hole at my favourite spot in the field.

Happiness is being fed my favourite cabbage veggies under the hot summer sun.

Happiness is tasting my sweet kale veggies when I am very hungry.

Happiness is sharing a piece of sweet kale with my very best friend.

Happiness is enjoying the big wide path scenery at this beach in the calm of the evening.

Happiness is again sharing this juicy piece of green kale with my best buddy.

Happiness is chewing on this soft veggie stalk under the cool tree shade on a warm summer afternoon.

Happiness is meeting with another curious visitor while I am exploring this huge grass field.

Happiness is being given a delicious treat when
I am hanging out among the dry sands searching
for one.

Happiness is savoring the freshness of this kale by this harsh thorny bush.

Happiness is getting this piece of lovely veggies
that is even sweeter than the blackberries.

Happiness is having something nice to munch on when I least expect it.

Happiness is discovering this piece of attractive kale right in front of my face when I am simply minding my own business.

Happiness is a piece of chewy banana for me while I am searching the ground.

Happiness is seeing so many apple slices and lettuce the first thing I wake up in the morning.

Happiness is sharing bright green veggies with my favourite neighbours.

Happiness is meeting another visitor when I am bored and curious...

Happiness is getting to know a visitor who does not mind how extremely plain-looking I am and still gives me plenty of veggies treat!

Happiness is spending another blessed week expecting and receiving the best from my God and His kind people. Until we meet again, may we find life's greatest treasures even when the days are boring and gray. My name is Gerry, a white bunny from Vancouver, greeting you all on behalf of my friends and siblings whom you saw featured in this book. Goodbye and God bless your day!

www.ingramcontent.com/pod-product-compliance
Lightning Source LLC
Chambersburg PA
CBHW041544260326
41914CB00015B/1543